WHEN THE MUSE CALLS

Poems for the Creative Life

WHEN THE MUSE CALLS

Poems for the Creative Life

Edited by
Kathryn Ridall

Pomegranate Press
California

Published by Pomegranate Press
El Sobrante, California.

Printed in the United States of America by BookMobile.
Distributed by Itasca.

Design by Roger Barry & Kathryn Ridall
Cover Art "The Poet" by Adrienne Amundsen
Photograph by Roger Barry

Library of Congress Control Number
2009941099

ISBN 978-0-692-00542-2

CONTENTS

INTRODUCTION

I. THE CALL

II. FROM SOMEWHERE ELSE

III. THE ROUND

IV. THE HONEY OF WORDS

V. THE NEED FOR SONG

VI.   SEEKING THE WORLD

VII. WITHOUT THE MUSE

VIII. MARGINS

IX. A COMMUNITY ACROSS TIME

INTRODUCTION

Many of us first heard about the dazzling beguiling muse when, as schoolchildren, we were taught about the Greek muses—nine goddesses, each embodying a domain of sacred activity and each inspiring humans to engage in that activity. We learned of the muses of poetry, dance, history, music, astronomy, comedy and tragedy. And many of us, including myself, concluded that a muse is an inspiration for people engaged in certain esoteric realms and that she has little interest in the rest of us.

Today, as a psychotherapist who has spent decades observing human creativity and as a poet who interacts intimately with a muse, I no longer agree with my youthful impressions. Although poets and artists may be more aware of daily interaction with their muse, and may pay more vocal homage to her, the muse dances through all lives. She inspires us to marry, have children, and build a career. She is present with gardeners and political activists, with cowboys and sailors. Wherever there is life, the luminous muse appears to inspire and lead us toward the next creative step on our life journey.

My first, powerful encounter with the muse occurred when I was nineteen and working for the State of Massachusetts as a mother's helper. One of my first assignments was in a rundown neighborhood of Boston.

Sheila, the woman I was sent to help, was an unemployed, single mother with a six month old son. She lived in a small apartment with windows facing a brick wall, and linoleum rolling away from the walls in cracked, yellowed strips. The sputtering refrigerator was almost empty. Sheila herself had a face that was seamed and ruined from years in barroom brawls.

Sheila's baby seemed healthy and alert—somewhat of a miracle in these grim circumstances. Equally surprising were the intricately crocheted afghans, vests, and pillows, piled neatly in every corner of the apartment. I particularly remember a champagne colored table cloth with exquisite, crimson roses. The furniture was spotted and listing but Sheila's eye for beauty was evident in her handiwork. I soon discovered that Sheila had her own diurnal cycle: days crocheting, nights in the bar.

No one encouraged Sheila to create these beautiful things. She had long since supplied her family with whatever she could convince them to take. She didn't make things to sell: she had no idea of their worth. She created her complex webs of yarn because she was driven to do so. The muse, with her insistent, incandescent passion, was deeply present in Sheila's hands and in her life.

This first encounter with the muse taught me that the muse inspires many different forms of creativity, not just dance or poetry. I learned that the muse is democratic, respecting neither social class nor finances. Most importantly, I saw that she can sweep a life up in her own passionate vortex, without regard for a person's conscious plans or self-concept.

Since that first unexpected introduction to the muse, I have observed her at work in the lives of friends and family. In my decades as a psychotherapist, my favorite moments have occurred when enough psychic pain is cleared that a person hears the call of his particular muse more clearly. I have seen lives transform as people begin to follow that call.

I resonate with the Swiss psychiatrist C. G. Jung who believed in s strong, lifelong drive toward wholeness or individuation. As we journey through life, our psychic DNA unfolds in a unique pattern, as many aspects of our self seek expression. Also like Jung, I believe in a deeper Self, that guides us through successive stages in our creative development. One way of understanding the muse is that she is the handmaiden of the Self, and that her inspiration guides us toward the next needed step in our development, whether that is a major life change or a poem we need to write.

In my own life, the muse has appeared many times— in romantic relationships, in my attraction to psychology, and in various spiritual explorations. Each time she has arrived in my life, she has catalyzed deep inner change and reshuffled my outer world.

When I was in my mid-fifties, I was restless and emotionally dry. My old psychological and spiritual pursuits no longer nurtured me but I was unable to find a new direction. Eventually I headed to a retreat center for a weekend with a transformational teacher. As it turned out, I had little affinity for that teacher but ten feet away, poet Robert Bly and Jungian analyst Marion Woodman were co-facilitating a workshop. I crossed those pivotal ten feet and Calliope, the muse of poetry, arrived in my life.

When I returned home after that weekend, Calliope, like any good muse, quickly turned my life upside down. Responding to her call, I replaced my old routines with new activities. I read and fell in love with poet after poet. I made lists of words and walked around my house sounding those words. I wrote, edited, and found mentors who taught me the craft of poetry. Eventually I began to submit my work and experienced exhilarating acceptances as well as disheartening rejections. When I lost contact with the muse, I felt flattened and sad.

From the beginning of my immersion in poetry, I collected poems written about poetry and the creative life. My life with Calliope was unanticipated and unsettling. When I found my experiences as a poet mirrored in the poetry of other poets, I felt comforted—I was on a recognizable path.

Although Calliope brought new experiences specific to poetry, I also recognized many parallels between relationship with this particular muse and experiences with other muses. As I read poetry about the creative life of poets, I felt that these poems would speak to lovers, parents, entrepreneurs, healers, artists, athletes, gardeners, and woodworkers—anyone engaged with a muse.

One of my favorite muse stories belongs to my friend Katya. At age twenty, Katya loved racquetball and was told that she had the talent to play the sport professionally. At that time, Katya didn't have the confidence or dedication to take on the discipline and challenges of a competitive sport. Although she competed some at the state level, she eventually turned away from athletics to become a successful social worker.

When Katya was in her early forties, the muse of racquetball returned in full force. This time Katya was ready for her. Katya began to play four or five days a week and cross-trained to develop her strength. She became one of the top players in her athletic club, competing with the strongest men. I once watched one of Katya's matches. Sweat poured from her as she flew around the court. Awed men whispered, "There's a ringer in there and it's a woman."

The muse is not to be treated lightly. She rises from our deepest unconscious longings and is fed by our insistent life force. If the muse doesn't capture us the first time around, she most likely will try again, as she did with Katya.

As I collected the poems in this volume, they began to cluster around repeating themes. The nine sections of this book reflect these themes. Everyone with a muse will recognize the often ecstatic, first call from a muse and how she brings inspiration from somewhere beyond the confines of our conscious awareness. Poems about the ongoing need for our creative passion and the despair when inspiration dries up will resonate with anyone who has loved a muse. Also familiar will be the desire to be validated for our labors, and the respect and love for others who have successfully walked the same path.

Some muses call to us and remain for a lifetime. Other muses are more transitory. They sweep us into their fiery arms and when we have completed a particular life task or goal, they drop us from their embrace. At any point in time, our life weaves together various creative passions, each with its own color and texture, its own focus and stage of development. When a formerly vibrant muse pales and vanishes, another muse may appear to guide us in new, unexpected directions.

The poems in this collection offer a window into the particular relationship of a poet with his muse. More importantly, they reveal much about living with any form of creative passion. Although our lives are filled with some-times overwhelming sorrow and loss, the muse resides within each of us, ready to inspire and guide us through our life journey.

THE CALL

Fires banked, windows rattling. We wander the world, hungry ghosts with uneasy sleep and a need for new life. Then she arrives—a lover, a pregnancy, an unanticipated form of work or play. The muse's guises are many, but her heart is always the same: blazing, beguiling, not to be denied.

POETRY

And it was at that age…poetry arrived
in search of me. I don't know, I don't know where
it came from, from winter or a river
I don't know how or when,
no, they weren't voices, they were not
words, nor silence,
but from a street it called me,
from the branches of the night,
abruptly from the others,
among raging fires
or returning alone,
there it was, without a face,
and it touched me.

I didn't know what to say, my mouth
had no way
with names,
my eyes were blind,
my soul,
fever or forgotten wings,
and I made my own way,
deciphering
that fire,
and I wrote the first, faint line,
faint, without substance, pure
nonsense,
pure wisdom
of one who knows nothing,
and suddenly I saw
the heavens
unfastened
and open,
planets,

palpitating plantations,
the darkness perforated,
riddled
with arrows, fires and flowers,
the overpowering night, the universe.

And I, tiny being,
drunk with the great starry
void,
likeness, image of
mystery,
felt myself a pure part
of the abyss,
I wheeled with the stars.
My heart broke loose with the wind.

Pablo Neruda
Translated by Alastair Reid

WHEN I MET MY MUSE

I glanced at her and took my glasses
off—they were still singing. They buzzed
like a locust on the coffee table and then
ceased. Her voice belled forth, and the
sunlight bent. I felt the ceiling arch, and
knew that nails up there took a new grip
on whatever they touched. "I am your own
way of looking a things," she said. "When
you allow me to live with you, every
glance at the world around you will be
a sort of salvation." And I took her hand.

William Stafford

WHEN I AM ASKED

When I am asked
how I began writing poems,
I talk about the indifference of nature.

It was soon after my mother died,
a brilliant June day,
everything blooming.

I sat on a gray stone bench
in a lovingly planted garden,
but the day lilies were as deaf
as the ears of drunken sleepers
and the roses curved inward.
Nothing was black or broken
and not a leaf fell
and the sun blared endless commercials
for summer holidays.

I sat on a gray stone bench
ringed with the ingenue faces
of pink and white impatiens
and placed my grief
in the mouth of language,
the only thing that would grieve with me.

Lisel Mueller

HOW I BECAME A POET

"Wanted" was the word I chose
for him at age eight, drawing the face
of a bad guy with comic-book whiskers
then showing it to my mother. This was how,

After my father left us, I made her smile
at the same time I told her I missed him,
and how I managed to keep him close by
in that house of perpetual anger,

becoming his accuser and his devoted
accomplice. I learned by writing
to negotiate between what I had,
and that more distant thing I dreamed of.

Welsey McNair

AWAKE

For fifty odd years I was rocked to sleep,
sucking my umbilical thumb. I held

my breath in the womb, dumb utterance
read by rote from the book of hours,

litany of chores shiny and clear as moral
imperatives, a book written

not by God, but a man not unlike the one
at the moment

demanding his breakfast. When I opened
my eyes the sun was a match

scratched into bloom with blue flame.
Neuron-knit synapse

and synapse and synapse, electric it came.
It came electric; in arc,

in surge, in high-voltage current. Now
beware. Sparks crackle my hair

and my fingertips smoke. I break, breathe
and burn. I learn my name.

Rebecca Foust

OLD WOMAN, YOUNG POET

I was old when poetry swept me up,
the same age Emily Dickinson died.

I see Emily and me, fifty-six
each of us, brushing elbows as we

pass one another by—her spirit,
quieted and complete, slides down

into the cool silences of the earth
while mine rises with sudden heat,

blossoms with the words she
is leaving behind. Others reborn

late might say, *What a miracle.*
Life arrives with such surprises

in her deep basket, and this may
be so—but what of the lost days,

months and years when the clay
of my dreaming self lay inert and

unshaped, when I knew nothing
of line breaks that pry open

the long heaviness of prose,
that allow a soul to finally sing?

Kathyrn Ridall

LOVE LIT A FIRE

Love lit a fire in my chest, and anything
that wasn't love left: intellectual
subtlety, philosophy
books, school.

All I want now
to do or hear
is poetry.

Rumi
Translated by Coleman Barks

FROM SOMEWHERE ELSE

A dream of the double helix and a poet's leaping image, a mother's sixth sense and the athlete's lift above matter—the muse bearing dazzling gifts from a dimly perceived inner sea.

THE MUSE

All that I am hangs by a thread tonight
as I wait for her whom no on can command.
Whatever I cherish most—youth, freedom, glory—
fades before her who bears the flute in her hand.

And look! she comes…she tosses back her veil,
staring me down, serene and pitiless.
"Are you the one," I ask, "whom Dante heard dictate
the lines of his *Inferno?*' She answers: "Yes."

                         Anna Akhmatova
                         Translated by Stanley Kunitz with
                         Max Hayward

ARS POETICA

At the edge of the forest
In the middle of the darkness
There is a hand,
As cold as copper,
Like a river
Stretched over wide stones.
Despite the hard rocks
And the furious wind
I love her
Like a flock of birds
Or a mild herd come to drink
For the exquisite rage
And sleek moss of her art.
There is something about a poem
That is violent
That is just another way to die,
Each time we realize our mysteries
We are weakened.
When I am writing I often scatter
Across a lascivious empire
Of passionate flowers.
They all seem so subversive
Even the ones with all their clothes on
They are so obsessed with the minute
Implications of who they are.
I believe if there is a struggle
It should go on
Where real lovers are.
I no longer regret
That I have smelted into one piece
For the sake of this poem.

Primus St. John

HOW POETRY COMES TO ME

It comes blundering over the
Boulders at night, it stays
Frightened outside the
Range of my campfire
I go to meet it at the
Edge of the light.

Gary Snyder

WHO

These lines are written
by an animal, an angel,
a stranger sitting in my chair;
by someone who already knows
how to live without trouble
among books, and pots and pans....

Who is it who asks me to find
language for the sound
a sheep's hoof makes when it strikes
a stone? And who speaks
the words which are my food?

Jane Kenyon

THE POEM

It discovers by night
what the day hid from it.
Sometimes it turns itself
into an animal.
In summer it takes long walks
by itself where meadows
fold back from ditches.
Once it stood still
in a quiet row of machines.
Who knows
what it is thinking?

Donald Hall

BUT

Out there in the large dark and in the long light is the breathless
Poem,
As ruthless and beautiful and amoral as the world is,
As nature is.

In the end there's just me and the bloody Poem and the murderous
Tongues of the trees,
Their glossy green syllables licking my mind (the green
Work of the wind).

Out there in the night between two trees is the Poem saying:
Do not hate me
Because I peeled the veil from your eyes and tore your world
To shreds, and brought

The darkness down upon your head. Here is a book of tongues,
Take it. (Dark leaves invade the air.)
Beware! Now I know a language so beautiful and lethal
My mouth bleeds when I speak it.

Gwendolyn MacEwen

M(OTHER) TONGUE

before...
when moon and stone
were the bulwark
against which   everything pushed
and blood
the first syllable
in the body's cup

when the pulse
at the base of the spine
was a seahorse
galloping

before Raven
tore open history's bag
or the equines rode
            the rock face of Lascaux

when time was the mind of the stars
as Pythagoras says
and the bright arms of motion
our first song

Julia Connor

THE NIGHT GARDEN

It is not in the sun-drenched fields
of your edited childhood. Nor
will you find it in the blown roses
running wild over the back gate. Instead
you must forsake the light, the easily
beautiful, and get down on your hands
and knees, down among the lilies
perspiring on their furred stems,
breathing the rare air of an otherworld
where shadow and moss-light and
a billion spores mingle in bluish vapors
that ferns tongue into their furled
centers, the sickly yellow slug
smears itself over roots in the gloom,
and tangled vines, slick with death,
trail their hypnotic blossoms through
the moist and pungent dark. It is here
that it dwells, under spotted fungi
with their skirts of poison, among
the cast-off husks of the dead, feeding
under cover and blooming in half-light,
astonishing issue of what we cannot know.

Mari L'Esperance

WHERE

Poetry hides
somewhere
behind the night of words
behind the clouds of hearing,
across the dark of sight,
and beyond the dusk of music
that's hidden and revealed.
But where is it concealed?
And how could I
possibly know
when I am
barely able,
by the light of day,
to find my pencil?

Taha Muhammad Ali
Translated by Peter Cole,
Yahya Hijazi & Gabriel Levin

VALENTINE FOR ERNEST MANN

You can't order a poem like you order a taco.
Walk up to the counter, say, "I'll take two"
and expect it to be handed back to you
on a shiny plate.

Still, I like your spirit.
Anyone who says, "Here's my address,
write me a poem," deserves something in reply.
So I'll tell a secret instead:
poems hide. In the bottoms of our shoes,
they are sleeping. They are the shadows
drifting across our ceilings the moment
before we wake up. What we have to do
is live in a way that lets us find them.

Once I knew a man who gave his wife
two skunks for a valentine.
He couldn't understand why she was crying.
"I thought they had such beautiful eyes."
And he was serious. He was a serious man
who lived in a serious way. Nothing was ugly
just because the world said so. He really
liked those skunks. So, he re-invented them
as valentines and they became beautiful.
At least, to him. And the poems that had been hiding
in the eyes of skunks for centuries
crawled out and curled up at his feet.

Maybe if we re-invent whatever our lives give us
we find poems. Check your garage, the odd sock
in your drawer, the person you almost like, but not quite.
And let me know.

Naomi Shihab Nye

THE ROUND

First white light exhilaration, our fingertips glow-
ing, but soon the muse demands her due: sleep
sacrificed to 4 a.m. feedings, old life abandoned
as the new lover settles in, a poet writing day and
night. The muse's bright burn served by rounds
of tribute.

THE ROUND

Light splashed this morning
on the shell-pink anemones
swaying on their tall stems;
down blue-spiked veronica
light flowed in rivulets
over the humps of the honeybees;
this morning I saw light kiss
the silk of the roses
in their second flowering,
my late bloomers
flushed with their brandy.
A curious gladness shook me.

So I have shut the doors of my house,
so I have trudged downstairs to my cell,
so I am sitting in semi-dark
hunched over my desk
with nothing for a view
to tempt me
but a bloated compost heap,
steamy old stinkpile,
under my window;
and I pick my notebook up
and I start to read aloud
the still-wet words I scribbled
on the blotted page:
"Light splashed…"

I can scarcely wait till tomorrow
when a new life begins for me,
as it does each day,
as it does each day.

Stanley Kunitz

DARK SUMMER DAYS

I have written my daughter to sleep,
she lies in the other bed among her books and toys,
the bowed and weathered instruments of her navigation.

In fragile possession of her course
and her own short set of ship's orders
she steps bravely out with me onto the burning waters.

We travel together, alone, in this single room
where the nails are growing out of the wood
and the paint flakes off the single window ledge;

on dark summer days when flying is difficult,
this is my Parisian garret, my narrow turret,
my writer's attic with its high beams and precious dust,

it is here I hunker down and shout into the dark,
some nights nothing, some nights
starbursts of language, jubilant in their release.

Across the fearless moon
hastens what little sky we can see; what few trees
stand in the mornings with their arms out,

through every time zone their same song
fills the loudness of our being alone,
together, in this gentle rocking of our seaglass room.

In her sleep, my girl is made of sand,
but at first light she's a young redwood
driving up like a mast through the sea foam;

and as for me, even if no words come
I'll be here waiting by the window in the predawn
before the birds.

Sara Tolchin

THE POETS ROOM

has nothing in it.
No comfortable furniture,
no TVs, voices,
clocks ticking, nothing
except beats of air and blood
pulsing through your lungs.

You take a clean breath
and quietness comes in.

Your favorite films start
flaring
on theatres of walls,
whenever
you are brave enough
to chase your images
with words.

In a future with few blank
walls,
libraries are hushed
museums,
where crowds devour your
books.
Others enter,
startled, tremulous.

Back to the Poets Room.
The bare room,
friendly in a dismal
daring way.

Here you can eat rocks,
jump precipices
and always recover, provided

you have pen and paper
to catch you.

Judith Pordon

HOW THESE WORDS HAPPENED

In winter, in the dark hours, when others
were asleep, I found these words and put them
together by their appetites and respect for
each other. In stillness, they jostled. They traded
meanings while pretending to have only one.

Monstrous alliances never dreamed of before
began. Sometimes they last. Never again
do they separate in this world. They die
together. They have a fidelity that no
purpose or pretense can ever break.

And all this happens like magic to the words
in those dark hours when others sleep.

William Stafford

POEMS SOMETIMES COME IN THE WAY
A SEA TURTLE LAYS HER EGGS

She heaves her way up from the sea,
hauls the heft
of her dark body
to keep an ancient promise;
when she comes to trust
the silence
she starts to dig:
flippers swat and scoop
a bowl,
grit flies back…
my bed is a white boat
she tell the moon's eye
as eggs
smooth as river stone
accumulate in sand.

Each turtle lays once,
then heads off
in the unruliness
of exhaustion
leaving the hidden nest
to uncertainty –
predators, weather –
but in time
under the slender auspices
of darkness,
hatchlings spill out,
the beach grass teems
with baby turtles
puzzling their awkward way
toward water,

shiny black bodies crawl
over each other
overflowing in the moonlight
so many, so small,
the first splash,
night and the ten thousand
new living things.

Susan Jackson

MAN WRITES POEM

This just in a man has begun writing a poem
in a small room in Brooklyn. His curtains
are apparently blowing in the breeze. We go now
to our man Harry on the scene, what's

the story down there Harry? "Well Chuck
he has begun the second stanza and seems
to be doing fine, he's using a blue pen, most
poets these days use blue or black ink so blue

is a fine choice. His curtains are indeed blowing
in a breeze of some kind and what's more his radiator
is 'whistling' somewhat. No metaphors have been
   written yet,
but I'm sure he's rummaging around down there

in the tin cans of his soul and will turn up something
for us soon. Hang on—just breaking news here Chuck,
there are 'birds singing' outside his window, and a car
with a bad muffler has just gone by. Yes...definitely

a confirmation on the singing birds." Excuse me Harry
but the poem seems to be taking on a very auditory quality
at this point wouldn't you say? "Yes Chuck, you're right,
but after years of experience I would hesitate to predict

exactly where this poem is going to go. Why I remember
being on the scene with Frost in '47, and with Stevens
   in `53,

and if there's one thing about poems these days it's that
hang on, something's happening here, he's just compared
   the curtains

to his mother, and he's described the radiator as 'Roaring
   deep
with the red walrus of History.' Now that's a key line,
especially appearing here, somewhat late in the poem,
when all of the similes are about to go home. In fact he
   seems

a bit knocked out with the effort of writing that line,
and who wouldn't be? Looks like…yes, he's put down
   his pen
and has gone to brush his teeth. Back to you, Chuck." Well
thanks Harry. Wow, the life of the artist. That's it for now,

but we'll keep you informed of more details as they arise.

Jay Leeming

THE OLD HEN

The old hen scratches
then looks, scratches then looks.
My life.

Jim Harrison and Ted Kooser

WORD GATHERING

She comes, an old woman
with the eyes of a kestrel

and her pin feathers are dappled
when she spreads her wings.

She has been out gathering words,
her pleasure and the spine of her life.

They hold her bones together with a minimum
of rattles. What else could she ask for?

In the rain, words have been easy
to find, settled like leaves along the path,

and besides, the more experienced nouns
know the old woman will be along.

Today she is looking for verbs, strong
with youth and blunt as hammers.

She'll gather them in armloads,
and carry them off in her cloak.

The woods are full of adjectives. She loves
their sounds, their bright lifting colors,

spends long hours admiring
their rolling descriptions, but the old woman

serves the poets, who have less use
for adjectives, seductive as they are.

When the poets come,
they jostle each other looking for words

both exact and new,
scoop huge piles and escape with them trailing.

Unchosen words rustle
around the old woman, nudging

her shoes, her hair, as she assures them
other poets will come.

CB Follett

THE HONEY OF WORDS

Taut lines and shimmering sails, the tremble of guitar strings and an infant's unimpeded gaze. Our muse's language—slow thick streams of honey.

SPEECH ALONE

It happens that one pronounces
a few words just for oneself
alone on this strange earth
then the small white flower
the pebble like all those that went before
the sprig of stubble
find themselves reunited
at the foot of the gate
which one opens slowly
to enter the house of clay
while chairs, table, cupboard,
blaze in a sun of glory.

Jean Follain
Translated by W.S. Merwin

SAYING THINGS (Excerpt)

Three things quickly – pineapple, sparrowgrass, whale –
and then on to asbestos. What I want to say tonight is
words, the naming of things into their thing,
yucca, brown sugar, solo, the roll of a snare drum,
say something, say anything, you'll see what I mean.
Say windmill, you feel the word fly out from under and away.
Say eye, say shearwater, alewife, apache, harpoon,
do you see what I'm saying, say celery, say Seattle,
say a whole city, say San Jose. You can feel the word
rising like a taste on the palate, say
tuning fork, angel, temperature, meadow, silver nitrate,
try carbon cycle, point lace, helium, Micronesia, quail.
Any word – say it – belladonna, screw auger, spitball,
any word goes like a gull up and on its way,
even lead lifts like a swallow from the nest
of your tongue. Say incandescence, bonnet, universal joint,
lint – oh I invite you to try it. Say cold cream,
corydalis, corset, cotillion, cosmic dust,
you are all of you a generous and patient audience,
pilaster, cashmere, mattress, Washington pie,
say vise, inclinometer, enjambment, you feel your own voice
taking off like a swift, when you say a word you feel like
a gong that's been struck, to speak is to step out of your skin,
stunned. And you're a pulsar, finally you understand light
is both particle and wave, you can see it, as in
parlour – when do you get a chance to say parlour –
and now mackinaw, toad, and ham wing their way
to the heaven of their thing. Say bellows, say sledge,

say threshold, cottonmouth, Russia leather,
say ash, picot, fallow deer, saxophone, say kitchen sink.
This is a birthday party for the mouth – it's better than ice
   cream...

Marilyn Krysl

THE WAY THE WALLS

The way the walls in this room
hold the sun's
warmth from yesterday until
today when the sky is
covered with clouds
I imagine
words have the
same ability to
save that
first radiance within
their blue
shadows

Annemette Kure Andersen
Translated by Thom Satterlee

WORDS

Words, like stars
linger above, offer a dream
of unvarnished truth

      kismet
          and   moira

vie to make sense of gases collapsed
into an endless static point
upon which we may pirouette

          perigee   or
     lunitidal

some word, please, to clarify
the force of our orbit, clouds wailing
around our ragged chunk of dirt

      plagioclase
         or   sapience

give us a means to describe light
as it pushes up, shattering
reforms in infinite strands

      refractometry   and
         fulgurate

a fusion of tongue more precise
than the religious texts that send us

hurling away from each other

     caritas
          odyl

lexicon, help us to locate gravity,
to converge upon ourselves,
into meaning.

Kirsten Jones Neff

THE PERFECT WORD

The perfect word
cuts,
glass shard
from a broken cup.
Burns
like coffee
gulped too fast
and repeats
indelible as sex
long into the morning after.
The perfect word,
wide-eyed seal,
watches through the water,
surfs
on every crest of inspiration.
Sleeps belly up and smiling
in the troughs.
The perfect word,
pearl slipped
one hungry mouth into another
melts unspoken
upon the tongue.

Jabez Willliam Churchill

EATING POETRY

Ink runs from the corners of my mouth.
There is no happiness like mine.
I have been eating poetry.

The librarian does not believe what she sees.
Her eyes are sad
and she walks with her hands in her dress.

The poems are gone.
The light is dim.
The dogs are on the basement stairs and coming up.

Their eyeballs roll,
their blond legs burn like brush.
The poor librarian begins to stamp her feet and weep.

She does not understand.
When I get on my knees and lick her hand,
she screams.

I am a new man.
I snarl at her and bark.
I romp with joy in the bookish dark.

Mark Strand

WORD DRUNK

I think of the twenty thousand poems of Li Po
and wonder, do words follow me or I them—
a word drunk?
I do not care about fine phrases,
the whoring after honor,
the stipend, the gift, the grant—
but I would feed on an essence
until it yields to me my own dumb form—
the weight raw, void of intent;
to see behind the clarity of my glass
the birth of new creatures
suffused with light.

Jim Harrison

THINKING OF TU FU'S POEM

I get up late and ask what has to be done today.
Nothing has to be done, so the farm looks doubly
   good.
The blowing maple leaves fit so well with the moving
   grass,
The shadow of my writing shack looks small beside
   the growing trees.

Never be with your children, let them get stringy like
   radishes!
Let your wife worry about the lack of money!
Your whole life is like a drunkard's dream!
You haven't combed your hair for a whole month!

Robert Bly

THE NEED FOR SONG

A brief sprint between two dark lakes, our suitcase heavy with fractured dreams. Our muse's song relieves the exhausted heart, helps us bear the cold white face of the moon.

SONNET TO ORPHEUS
Part One
XIX

As swiftly as the world is changing,
like racing clouds,
all that is finished
falls home to the ancient source.

Above the change and the loss,
farther and freer,
your singing continues,
god of the lyre.

How can we embrace our sorrows
or learn how to love,
or see what we lose

when we die? Only your song
over the earth
honors our life and makes it holy.

Rainer Maria Rilke
Translated by Anita Barrows
& Joanna Macy

YOU'D SING TOO

You'd sing too
if you found yourself
in a place like this
You wouldn't worry about
whether you were as good
as Ray Charles or Edith Piaf
You'd sing
You'd sing
not for yourself
but to made a self
out of the old food
rotting in the astral bowel
and the loveless thud
of your own breathing
You'd become a singer
faster than it takes
to hate a rival's charm
and you'd sing, darling
you'd sing too

Leonard Cohen

SIGN YOUR NAME

on a scrap of paper,
crumple or tear it up and throw it away:

that's how the world works, friend.
Maybe you can't even get as far

as gripping a pen, maybe your hand
is scrabbling in a few dirty grains

of rice, or you're licking a tin plate
or just your fly-crawled lips. Welcome

and farewell: you're stacked or stashed
or set aflame, turning on the spit,

the axis, the long pole that runs
through everyone. If you're here

you're already nearly gone. Write
if you can. If you can, give us a song.

Kim Addonizio

BREAK THE RULES

Be rock, paper, scissors.
Shout. Smack your hands
against the grain of air
in shapes of fist-hand,
open-hand, two-fingers-out.
Watch rock smash scissors,
scissors cut paper. Never
let your paper die. Catch
fire. Burn hot enough
to crack rock, melt scissors
into nickel, iron, manganese.
And stay cool. Dig down.
Seek your water. Give it
time enough to sink rock,
rust scissors, soak paper
back to pulp, wood, trees.
Pull yourself up by the roots.
Walk them to the edge.
Tell it out a river's mouth.
Wade deep into your sea.
Flail. Drown. Do anything
to taste salt. Make waves.

William Keener

IN THE WARM FOLDS

I leave the warm folds of my bed's embrace
for some unremembered chore
cool air wraps me in goosebumps
hurries my step

crawling back into the featherbed softness
nearly forgotten in the cool journey
I am re-embraced by my own recent warmth
feel myself re-entering my own skin
my own life-force breathing life back into
the chilled pilgrim I had become

this is why I write:
to be amazed by my own fire

this is why I read:
to crawl briefly into yours

Vilma Olsvary Ginzberg

MY SUFFERING

My suffering
is useful to me.

It gives me the privilege
to write on the suffering of others.

My suffering is a pencil
with which I write.

Anna Swir
*Translated by Czeslaw Milosz
& Leonard Nathan*

WHAT ISSA HEARD

Two hundred years ago Issa heard the morning birds
singing sutras to this suffering world.

I heard them too, his morning, which must mean,

since we will always have a suffering world,
we must also always have a song.

David Budbill

BABY WRENS' VOICES

I am a student of wrens.
When the mother bird returns
to her brood, beak squirming
with winged breakfast, a shrill
clamor rises like jingling
from tiny, high-pitched bells.
Who'd have guessed such a small
house contained so many voices?
The sound they make is the pure sound
of life's hunger. Who hangs our house
in the world's branches, and listens
when we sing from our hunger?
Because I love best those songs
that shake the house of the singer,
I am a student of wrens.

Thomas R. Smith

LAKE AND MAPLE

I want to give myself
utterly
as this maple
that burned and burned
for three days without stinting
and then in two more
dropped every leaf;
as this lake that,
no matter what comes
to its green-blue depths,
both takes and returns it.
In the still heart,
that refuses nothing,
the world is twice-born—
two earths wheeling,
two heavens,
two egrets reaching
down into subtraction;
even the fish
for an instant doubled,
before it is gone.
I want the fish.
I want the losing it all
when it rains and I want
the returning transparence.
I want the place
by the edge-flowers where
the shallow sand is deceptive,
where whatever
steps in must plunge,
and I want that plunging.
I want the ones
who come in secret to drink

only in early darkness,
and I want the ones
who are swallowed.
I want the way
this water sees without eyes,
hears without ears,
shivers without will or fear
at the gentlest touch.
I want the way it
accepts the cold moonlight
and lets it pass,
the way it lets
all of it pass
without judgment or comment.
There is a lake,
Lalla Ded sang, no larger
than one seed of mustard,
that all things return to.
O heart, if you
will not, cannot, give me the lake,
then give me the song.

Jane Hirshfield

BIRDSONG BRINGS RELIEF

Birdsong brings relief
to my longing.

I am just as ecstatic as they are,
but with nothing to say!

Please, universal soul, practice
some song, or something, through me!

Rumi
Translated by Coleman Barks

SEEKING THE WORLD

In season, the muse's seeds drift toward earth. Sometimes seeds take hold and spring arrives with her cape of roses and lilacs and sometimes seeds disappear into soil, dark and indifferent.

THIS IS MY LETTER TO THE WORLD

This is my letter to the World
That never wrote to Me -
The simple News that Nature told -
With tender Majesty

Her Message is committed
To Hands I cannot see -
For love of Her – Sweet – countrymen -
Judge tenderly - of Me

Emily Dickinson

DEAR READER

I am trying to pry open your casket
with this burning snowflake.

I'll give up my sleep for you.
This freezing sleet keeps coming down
and I can barely see.

If this trick works we can rub our hands
together, maybe

start a little fire
with our identification papers.
I don't know but I keep working, working

half hating you,
half eaten by the moon.

James Tate

FAME IS A BEE

Fame is a bee.
It has a song—
It has a sting—
Ah, too, it has a wing.

Emily Dickinson

THE SECRET

Two girls discover
the secret of life
in a sudden line of
poetry.

I who don't know the
secret wrote
the line. They
told me

(through a third person)
they had found it
but not what it was
not even

what line it was. No doubt
by now, more than a week
later, they have forgotten
the secret,

the line, the name of
the poem. I love them
for finding what
I can't find,

and for loving me
for the line I wrote,
and for forgetting it
so that

a thousand times, till death
finds them, they may
discover it again, in other
lines

in other
happenings. And for
wanting to know it,
for

assuming there is
such a secret, yes,
for that
most of all.

Denise Levertov

POETRY READING

To be a boxer, or not to be there
at all. O Muse, where are *our* teeming crowds?
Twelve people in the room, eight seats to spare—
it's time to start this cultural affair.
Half came inside because it started raining,
the rest are relatives. O Muse.

The women here would love to rant and rave,
but that's for boxing. Here they must behave.
Dante's Inferno is ringside nowadays.
Likewise his Paradise. O Muse.

Oh, not to be a boxer but a poet,
one sentenced to hard shelleying for life,
for lack of muscles forced to show the world
the sonnet that may make the high-school reading lists
with luck. O Muse,
O bobtailed angel, Pegasus.

In the first row, a sweet old man's soft snore:
he dreams his wife's alive again. What's more,
she's making him that tart she used to bake.
Aflame, but carefully—don't burn his cake!—
we start to read. O Muse.

Wislawa Szymborska
Translated by Stanislaw Baranczak
& Clare Cavnaugh

70

POETRY READING

I'm curled into a ball
like a dog
that is cold.

Who will tell me
why I was born,
why this monstrosity
called life.

The telephone rings. I have to give
a poetry reading.

I enter.
A hundred people, a hundred pairs of eyes.
They look, they wait.
I know for what.

I am supposed to tell them
why they were born,
why there is
this monstrosity called life.

Anna Swir
*Translated by Czeslaw Milosz
& Leonard Nathan*

MIGHTY STRONG POEMS

for Billy Collins

"What mighty strong poems," he said.
And I repeat it all day, staggering
under sheaves of rejections.
But my poems, oh yes, they are brawny.
Even now I can see them working out at the gym
in their tiny leopard leotards, their muscly words
glazed with sweat. They are bench pressing
heavy symbolism. Heaving stacks of similes,
wide-stanced and grimacing. Some try so hard,
though it's a lost cause. Their wrinkled syntax,
no matter how many reps they do, will sag.
But doggedly, they jog in iambic pentameter,
Walkmans bouncing. Some glisten with clever
enjambments, end rhymes tight as green plums.
Others practice caesuras in old sweats.
But they're all there, huffing and puffing,
trying their best. Even the babies, the tender
first-drafts, struggling just to turn over, whimpering
in frustration. None of them give up.
Not the short squat little haikus
or the alexandrines trailing their long, graceful
Isadora Duncan lines. While I fidget
by the mailbox, they sail off in paper airplanes,
brave as kindergartners boarding the school bus.
They're undaunted in their innocent conviction,
their heartbreaking hope. They want to lift cars
off pinned children, rescue lost and frozen
wanderers—they'd bound out,
little whiskey barrels strapped to their necks.

They dream of shrugging off their satin
warm-up robes and wrestling with evil.
They'd hoist the sack of ordinary days
and bear it aloft like a crown. They believe
they're needed. Even at night when I sleep
and it looks like they're sleeping, they're still
at it, lying silently on the white page,
doing isometrics in the dark.

Ellen Bass

MY FIRST BOOK OF POETRY
WAS LIKE MY FIRST BABY

since I don't plan to have children. I wanted people to love it
and make a fuss, and, in turn, tell me what a great job I'd done.
My book wasn't reviewed in that many places, and when it was,
one reviewer even called it sloppy. The grandparents weren't
    as doting
as I'd expected. They went on with their own lives
and didn't buy the book any presents. No one took a picture
    of me
holding the book in my lap. My husband wasn't jealous
that I was spending too much time with the book. My dog
sniffed the book and walked away, unthreatened. Other
    books
were getting cooed and fussed over, books cuter and more
    enchanting than mine.
There is no greater pain for a mother--seeing her child left
    out. Soon I knew
I had a book that would never accomplish much with its life,
that it wouldn't win prizes or be displayed in prestigious
    bookstores.
That my book would probably be a drop-out, that I'd have
    nothing
to brag about when my cousins showed me graduation
    pictures of their kids.
That my book wouldn't buy me dinner or take care of me
when I grew old. I tried not to let the book sense my
    disappointment.
I tried to love it for the book that it was, but it began to
    have the telltale signs
of depression, hanging out with the wrong crowd,

dressing like a rebel. The book reminded me of myself as a
    teenager,
but when I told it that it shivered in disgust, blaming me
for bringing it into this world in the first place.

Denise Duhamel

WITHOUT THE MUSE

The sky an orange and red savannah, lavender clouds roaming her plains—the one with greater vision is with us. When she vanishes, horizons collapse to a single line, clouds fall into the sea.

ALL HAS BEEN TAKEN AWAY

All has been taken away: strength and love.
My body, cast into an unloved city,
is not glad of the sun. I feel my blood
has gone quite cold in me.

I'm baffled by the Muse's state of mind:
she looks at me and doesn't say a word,
and lays her head, in its dark wreath,
exhausted, on my breast.

And only conscience, more terribly each day
rages, demanding vast tribute.
For answer I hide my face in my hands...
but I have run out of tears and excuses.

Anna Akhmatova
*Translated by Stanley Kunitz with
Max Hayward*

NOT WRITING

A wasp rises to its papery
nest under the eaves
where it daubs

at the gray shape,
but seems unable
to enter its own house.

Jane Kenyon

SONG FOR THE SALMON

For too many days now I have not written of the sea,
nor the rivers, nor the shifting currents
we find between the islands.

For too many nights now I have not imagined the salmon
threading the dark streams of reflected stars,
nor have I dreamt of his longing
nor the lithe swing of his tail toward dawn.

I have not given myself to the depth to which he goes,
to the cargoes of crystal water, cold with salt,
nor the enormous plains of ocean swaying beneath the
   moon.

I have not felt the lifted arms of the ocean
opening its white hands on the seashore,
nor the salted wind, whole and healthy
filling the chest with living air.

I have not heard those waves
fallen out of heaven onto earth,
nor the tumult of sound and the satisfaction
of a thousand miles of ocean
giving up its strength on the sand.

But now I have spoken of that great sea,
the ocean of longing shifts through me,
the blessed inner star of navigation
moves in the dark sky above

and I am ready like the young salmon
to leave his river, blessed with hunger
for a great journey on the drawing tide.

David Whyte

SUMMONED

she's a petulant,
reluctant,
ineloquent muse

a complaining,
refraining,
and waning muse

who resists caress,
unimpressed by your
lavender candle,

and new pen set,
the darkened room,
your vision quest

or other ruse; she'll
refuse you every time
you ask. But when

she comes unbidden
and barefoot, hair
unbound, her kisses

are rain, and she tastes
like sound, like oak
in wine, like time

and shame and wet
on wood, like sun on snow.
Then she pulls you
down like undertow.

Rebecca Foust

MADMEN

They say you can jinx a poem
if you talk about it before it is done.
If you let it out too early, they warn,
your poem will fly away,
and this time they are absolutely right.

Take the night I mentioned to you
I wanted to write about the madmen,
as the newspapers so blithely call them,
who attack art, not in reviews,
but with breadknives and hammers
in the quiet museums of Prague and Amsterdam.

Actually, they are the real artists,
you said, spinning the ice in your glass.
The screwdriver is their brush.
The restorers are the true vandals,
you went on, slowly turning me upside-down,
the ones in the white smocks
always closing the wound in the landscape
and ruining the art of the mad.

I watched my poem fly down to the front
of the bar and hover there
until the next customer walked in—
then I watched it fly out the door into the night
and sail away, I could only imagine,
over the dark tenements of the city.

All I had wished to say
was that art, too, was short,
as a razor can teach with a blind slash;
it only seems long when you compare it to life,

but that night I drove home alone
with nothing swinging in the cage of my heart
but the faint hope that I might catch
in the fan of my headlights
a glimpse of the thing,
maybe perched on a road sign or a streetlamp—
poor unwritten bird, its wings folded,
staring down at me with tiny illuminated eyes.

Billy Collins

BEGGAR

The Muse came dragging her carpetbag of woes.
Heaped herself on the back step, her boots unlaced,
skirts dusty, torn—nothing Greek or ethereal
about her. She was missing some teeth, her hair

had gone unwashed for weeks. Hardly an inspiration,
I thought, as I offered her water. She gulped
as if her thirst were one with the drought afflicting
the area. Then she shut her eyes, rubbed her throat.

A sign for me to leave her alone? find words
on my own? I can't say. I left her sleeping
in the sun; by evening, she was gone. That night
every star I saw turned into a word and the sky

filled with fiery poems that burned their way
into the eternal. The silence when I woke
seemed more bearable, a gift I knew
I should take for what it was: air, pure air.

Lynne Knight

UNDOING A POEM

Start from the end and peel back meaning
Word by word, line by line
Undress each stanza like it was a virgin
Slowly, carefully
Unraveling metaphor until it extinguishes itself
Falls away from the dim rooms of conscious thought

Tear away the flesh of imagery
Until it lies alone inside your shallow breath
Gaping open like the uncut truth

Shave down the meter, sweep it into small piles
With the unread verse
And repeat to yourself the untraceable words
That remain scattered inside you

Deconstruct language from your very being
Until you are alone in a room
Left with a scaffolding of blank pages

Fall to your knees

Grope the fallible floor for the framework of phraseology
Until you fall back onto one rusty nail
Then bleed backwards into the placenta
To the place where you found yourself
Absent of all language
Again

Connie Post

MARGINS

Our most luminous muse has her limits and we
stand alone in chilling winds—the universe with
its empty borders, the inscrutable sea with
margins of sand and stone.

POET IN THE CITY OF FEAR

The only dancers in the City of Fear
are wooden. They clunk along the broken
streets, pointing the way with their elbows.

The city builders are crazed—haphazard
scaffolding, wrecking balls and cranes.
Their teetering towers of mirrored glass.

The trees in the city are full of monkeys,
air a smudge of smoke and ash;
the brown rivers bob with debris.

The only poet in the City of Fear
is dumb and almost blind. He sleeps
among the rubble, but sometimes

a dusty hum rolls out of him, down the hill.
There's another world, you can almost
hear it say. *Beyond the wall and muddy river.*

*It is a land of flow and flutter, of dragon fruit
and long-tailed birds. Wild things grow up from
the ground. Things can flower there—even words.*

Pratho Sereno

THE IMAGE-MAKER

A wind passed over my mind,
insidious and cold.
It is a thought, I thought,
but it was only its shadow.
Words came,
or the breath of my sisters,
with a black rustle of wings.
They came with a summons
that followed a blessing.
I could not believe
I too would be punished.
Perhaps it is time to go,
to slip alone, as at a birth,
out of this glowing house
where all my children danced.
Seductive Night! I have stood
at my casement the longest hour,
watching the acid wafer
of the moon slowly dissolving
in a scud of cloud, and heard
the farthest hidden stars
calling my name.
I listen, but I avert my ears
from Meister Eckhart's warning:
All things must be forsaken.
God scorns
to show Himself among images.

Stanley Kunitz

ARCHAEOLOGY

'Our real poems are already in us
and all we can do is dig.'—Jonathan Galassi

You knew the odds on failure from the start,
that morning you first saw, or thought you saw,
beneath the heartstruck plains of a second-rate country
the outline of buried cities. A thousand to one
you'd turn up nothing more than the rubbish heap
of a poor Near Eastern backwater:
a few chipped beads,
splinters of glass and pottery, broken tablets
whose secret lore, laboriously deciphered,
would prove to be only a collection of ancient grocery lists.
Still, the train moved away from the station without you.

How many lives ago
was that? How many choices?
Now that you've got your bushelful of shards
do you say, *give me back my years*
or wrap yourself in the distant
glitter of desert stars,
telling yourself it was foolish after all
to have dreamed of uncovering
some fluent vessel, the bronze head of a god?
Pack up your fragments. Let the simoom
flatten the digging site. Now come
the passionate midnights in the museum basement
when out of that random rubble you'll invent

the dusty market smelling of sheep and spices,
streets, palmy gardens, courtyards set with wells
to which, in the blue of evening, one by one
come strong veiled women, bearing their perfect jars.

Katha Pollitt

READING CHINESE POETRY
BEFORE DAWN

Sleepless again,
I get up.
A cold rain
beats at the windows.
Holding my coffee,
I ponder Tu Fu's
overturned wine glass.
At his window, snow,
twelve hundred years fallen;
under his hand,
black ink not yet dry.
"Letters are useless."
The poet is old, alone,
his woodstove is empty.
The fame of centuries
casts off no heat.
In his verse, I know,
is a discipline
lost to translation;
here, only the blizzard remains.

Jane Hirshfield

IN HIDING

I look at the mountain from the window,
it does not see me.
I hide, I write a poem,
not that it matters,
and I see the old grace. It is useless.
As before, the moon cuts into the sky
and the cherry opens.

Miklós Radnóti
Translated by Stephen Berg,
S. S. Marks, and Steven Polgar

WHERE GOES HER SONG

when the bright blue bay   the golden bridge are ripped
    from her eyes
when her face is lost to the gaze of the sun
where will her morning devotions go   who will sit on this
    wooden porch
ponder the inward valley   make marks on white paper

when her face is lost to the gaze of the sun
when the eye of the sky   has forgotten her name
who will ponder the inward valley   make black marks on
    paper
where goes her song   her lamentation   her prayer

when the eye of the sky has forgotten her name
will anyone read these words
where goes her song   her lamentation   her prayer
the eyes of her love with their yellow glint

will anyone read these words
where go Sofia   Jerusalem   Calcutta
the eyes of her love with their yellow glint
cities   temples   flesh   torn out of memories membranes

where go Sofia   Jerusalem   Calcutta
the eyes of that beggar   his shriveled up hand in Bombay
cities   temples   flesh   torn out of memories membranes
the red lotus   the butter ball   what she offered to Kali

the eyes of the beggar   his shriveled up hand in Bombay
she will become whatever one is after breath
red lotus   butter ball   an offering to Kali
ah! she will miss how the morning light falls into the valley

when she becomes whatever one is after breath
where will her morning devotions go   who will there be on
    this wooden porch
ah! she will miss how the morning light falls into the valley
when the bright blue bay   the golden bridge are ripped
    from her eyes

Naomi Ruth Lowinsky

A COMMUNITY ACROSS TIME

She leads us on a road that soars, dips, swerves, and disappears. How we cherish others who sing and weep under the same star—those who came before, those who travel with us now, and those who will follow when we are gone.

LEAVING THE TEMPLE IN NIMES

And, sure enough,
I came face to face with the spring.
Down in the wet darkness of the winter moss
Still gathering in the Temple of Diana,
I came to the trunk of a huge umbrella pine
Vivid and ancient as always,
Among the shaped stones.
I couldn't see the top of the branches,
I stood down there in the pathway so deep.
But a vine held its living leaves all the way down
To my hands. So I carry away with me
Four ivy leaves:

In gratitude to the tall pale girl
Who still walks somewhere behind the pine tree,
Slender as her hounds.
In honor of the solitary poet,
Ausonius, adorer of the southern hillsides
Who drank of this sacred spring
Before he entered this very holy place
And slowly turned the passionate silver
Of his Latin along the waters.

And I will send one ivy leaf, green in winter,
Home to an American girl I know.
I caught a glimpse of her once in a dream,
Shaking out her dark and adventurous hair.
She revealed only a little of her face
Through the armful of pussy willow she gathered
Alive in spring,
Alive along the Schuylkill in Philadelphia.

She will carry this ivy leaf from Diana's pine
As she looks toward Camden, across the river,
Where Walt Whitman, the chaste wanderer
Among the live-oaks, the rain, railyards and battlefields,
Lifts up his lovely face
To the moon and allows it to become
A friendly ruin.
The innocent huntress will come down after dark,
Brush the train smoke aside, and leave alone together
The old man rooted in an ugly place
Pure with his lovingkindness,
And a girl with an ivy leaf revealing her face
Among fallen pussy willow.

James Wright

TONIGHT I AM IN LOVE

Tonight, I am in love with poetry,
with the good words that saved me,
with the men and women who
uncapped their pens and laid the ink
on the blank canvas of the page.

I am shameless in my love; their faces
rising on the smoke and dust at the end
of day, their sullen eyes and crusty hearts,
the murky serum now turned to chalk
along the gone cords of their spines.

I'm reciting the first anonymous lines
that broke night's thin shell: *sonne under wode.*
A baby is born us bliss to bring. I have labored
sore and suffered death. Jesus' wounds so wide.

I am wounded with tenderness for all who labored
in dim rooms with their handful of words,
battering their full hearts against the moon.

They flee from me that sometime did me seek.
Wake, now my love, awake: for it is time.
For God's sake hold your tongue and let me love!

What can I do but love them? Sore throated
they call from beneath blankets of grass,
through the wind-torn elms, near the river's
edge, voices shorn of everything but the one
hope, the last question, the first loss, calling

Slow, slow, fresh fount, keep time with my salt tears.
Whenas in silks my Julia goes, calling *Why do I*
languish thus, drooping and dull as if I were all earth?

Now they are bones, the sweet ones who once
considered a cat, a nightingale, a hare, a lamb,
a fly, who saw a Tyger burning, who passed
five summers and five long winters, passed them
and saved them and gave them away in poems.

They could not have known how I would love them,
worlds fallen from their mortal fingers.
When I cannot see to read or walk alone
along the slough, I will hear you, I will
bring the longing in your voices to rest
against my old, tired heart and call you back.

Dorianne Laux

A NEW POET

Finding a new poet
is like finding a new wildflower
out in the woods. You don't see

its name in the flower books, and
nobody you tell believes
in its odd color or the way

its leaves grow in splayed rows
down the whole length of the page. In fact
the very page smells of spilled

red wine and the mustiness of the sea
on a foggy day—the odor of truth
and of lying.

And the words are so familiar,
so strangely new, words
you almost wrote yourself, if only

in your dreams there had been a pencil
or a pen or even a paintbrush,
if only there had been a flower.

Linda Pastan

MY POETS

The first is called Gonzalo de Berceo,
Gonzalo de Berceo, pilgrim and poet,
who on a pilgrimage happened on a meadow.
Sages paint him copying a manuscript.

He sang to Saint Domingo, sang to Mary,
to Saints Millán, Lorenzo, Oria. But he
said: My narration's not mere jongleury.
I wrote it down and it's true history.

His verse is soft and grave, monotonous rows
of winter poplars in which nothing shines;
his lines are furrows where dark seeds repose
and far Castilian mountains with blue pines.

Copying old tales which are in candor dressed,
reading the lives of saints and books of prayer,
he tells us where the weary pilgrims rest
while his heart's light emerges in the air.

Antonio Machado
Translated by Willis Barnstone

AMERICAN POET,
WILLIAM STAFFORD, 1914-1993

If he were a landscape, we'd call him ordinary:
plain and dusty, flat except for a few low hills,
a few surviving pines, a scatter of yellow rabbitbush,
in several shades of brown—
the sort of place we'd hardly call a place
in our hurry down the highway,
never to wonder how it was
the trees got placed just so.

If we got out and walked around,
we'd find, in season, marvelous belly flowers
echoing the stars, but in Technicolor
and full of seeds, and there,
behind that slope of tawny grass,
a spring up-welling, clear and cold!
So cold it stings our hands and lips to life.
When the light sinks low, we'd see
sharp shadows of the Cascade Range
perfect their peaks across his back.

If there were miners wandering by,
those who knew how to dig and where,
they'd discover for us
what we might have found for ourselves:
imperishable rivers of gold below.

Don Emblen

MOURNING PABLO NERUDA

Water is practical,
Especially in
August.
Faucet water
That drops
Into the buckets
I carry
To the young
Willow trees
Whose leaves have been eaten
Off by grasshoppers.
Or this jar of water
That lies next to me
On the car seat
As I drive to my shack.
When I look down,
The seat all
Around the jar
Is dark,
For water doesn't intend
To give, it gives
Anyway,
And the jar of water
Lies
There quivering
As I drive
Through a countryside
Of granite quarries,
Stones
Soon to be shaped
Into blocks for the dead,
The only

Thing they have
Left that is theirs.

For the dead remain inside
Us, as water
Remains
Inside granite—
Hardly at all—
For their job is to
Go
Away,
And not come back,
Even when we ask them,
But water
Comes to us—
It doesn't care
About us, it goes
Around us, on the way
To the Minnesota River,
To the Mississippi River,
To the Gulf,
Always closer
To where
It has to be.
No one lays flowers
On the grave
Of water,
For it is not
Here,
It is
Gone.

Robert Bly

SEPTEMBER 1961

This is the year the old ones,
the old great ones
leave us alone on the road.

The road leads to the sea.
We have the words in our pockets,
obscure directions. The old ones

have taken away the light of their presence,
we see it moving away over a hill
off to one side.

They are not dying,
they are withdrawn
into a painful privacy

Learning to live without words.
E.P. "It looks like dying"— Williams: "I can't
describe to you what has been

happening to me"—
H.D. "unable to speak."
The darkness

twists itself in the wind, the stars
are small, the horizon
ringed with confused urban light-haze.

They have told us
the road leads to the sea,
and given

the language into our hands.
We hear
our footsteps each time a truck

has dazzled past us and gone
leaving us new silence.
One can't reach

the sea on this endless
road to the sea unless
one turns aside at the end, it seems,

follows
the owl that silently glides above it
aslant, back and forth,

 and away into deep woods.

But for us the road
unfurls itself, we count the
words in our pockets, we wonder

how it will be without them, we don't
stop walking, we know
there is far to go, sometimes

we think the night wind carries
a smell of the sea...

Denise Levertov

LATE NIGHT, YEAR'S END,
DOING THE BOOKS WITH TU FU

For Sam Hammill

Ghost fires in the jade palace. Moonlight
a scattering of opals on the river. Over us
beasts of the zodiac march across the night.
We drink cup after cup of warm rice wine.
It's time to take out the ledger, to figure
the year's accounts. Tu Fu, if our days
and nights are the principal, if all the years
are interest, then how much do we owe?
If I subtract my grief from joy, what is left?
Tell me, old friend, how does it balance?
In one of your last poems you talk about
the stars outside your hut, how impossible
to count them. *There are no numbers,*
you say, *for this life. Who cares if we're*
in the red? Or the black? Add a few zeros,
and we're rich. Erase a few, and we're poor.
You're right, Tu Fu. Rich or poor, the night
each night burgeons within us. The mornings
open with sunlight. Why count them?
Instead of numbers, let me enter words
into the ledger, this account of our friendship,
this little poem from me to you, across
the glimmering, innumerable years.

Joseph Stroud

WITH THANKS

To Adrienne Amundsen for contributing "The Poet" to the cover art of this book and for her attentive editing suggestions.

To Lynn Ireland and Wilma Friesema for unwavering support and for helpful editing suggestions.

To Thomas R. Smith for help with the technicalities of putting together an anthology and early editing suggestions.

To Mari L'Esperance for her careful proofreading of the poems.

To Barbara McEnerney, with special thanks, for suggesting poems, using her library skills to track down the credits for many poems, and for editing advice.

To my husband Roger Barry for daily encouragement and for being the photographer and the publisher of this book.

And finally to all the poets who kindly allowed me to publish their work without a fee and to the publishing houses that provided reduced fees. Thank you.

THE POETS

KIM ADDONIZIO (b.1954) was born in Washington, DC. A novelist and author of five books of poetry, she also has published two instructional books on poetry: THE POET'S COMPANION (with Dorianne Laux) and ORDINARY GENIUS. Known for her edgy, emotionally honest voice, she has been awarded two fellowships from the National Endowment for the Arts, a Guggenheim Fellowship, a Pushcart Prize, and a Commonwealth Club Poetry Medal. She lives in Oakland, California where she teaches ongoing poetry workshops.

ANNA AKHMATOVA (1889-1966) was born in Odessa, Russia. She began writing at 14 and published her first book in 1912. As an artist in Stalinist Russia, she suffered many hardships including an official ban on her work and the death of loved ones in prison. Akhmatova's themes include love and loss, the challenge of being a creative woman, and the difficulties of living and writing under a dictatorship. Toward the end of her life, the ban on her work was lifted and she was allowed to travel to receive international honors.

TAHA MUHAMMAD ALI (b.1931) was born in Saffuriyya in Galilee. In 1948 his family fled to Lebanon during the Arab-Israeli War. A year later, they returned to Nazareth where he still lives. He has made his living as owner of a souvenir/antique store while writing short stories and poetry about the political upheavals he has experienced.

ANNEMETTE KURE ANDERSEN (b.1962) was born in Ribe in South Jutland, Denmark. She is a poet, translator, and editor of the influential journal HVDEKORN (Whealtgrains) from 1996-2001. She has translated Italian poets as well as written herself of Italian landscapes. She is best known for short poems, closely aligned with Japanese haiku.

ELLEN BASS (b.1947), born in Philadelphia, has published several books of poetry including MULES OF LOVE which won the Lambda Literary Award. Her many awards include the Nimrod/ Hardman Pablo Neruda Prize and a Fellowship from the California Arts Council. She teaches in the low residency MFA program at Pacific University and at other locations nationally and internationally. She lives in Santa Cruz, California.

ROBERT BLY (b.1926) was born in Minnesota to parents of Norwegian ancestry. His many roles have included poet, editor, translator, political activist, and founder of the expressive men's movement. His literary journals, THE FIFTIES, THE SIXTIES, and THE SEVENTIES brought European and Latin American poetry to the attention of the American literary world. He has published over 30 books of poetry and several books of nonfiction. His many awards include the National Book Award and National Endowment for the Arts and Guggenheim Fellowships.

DAVID BUDBILL (b.1940) was born in Cleveland, Ohio. He is the author of seven books of poems, eight plays, and many short stories and essays. In 2003, he released SONG OF A SUFFER-ING WORLD: A PRAYER FOR PEACE, A PROTEST AGAINST WAR with William Parker and Harold Decker. His many honors include National Endowment for the Arts and Guggenheim Fellowships. In 2002 the Vermont Arts Council granted him an award for lifetime achievement in the arts.

JABEZ WILLIAM CHURCHILL (b.1951) was born in Santa Rosa, California. A celebrant of languages, he writes primarily in English and Spanish but occasionally in French and Greek. He has published four chapbooks and a trilingual manuscript OUT-SIDER IN THE AMERICAS. He lives in Ukiah, California.

LEONARD COHEN (b.1934), born in Montreal, is best known as an influential singer-songwriter. He is also a poet and novelist. His most recent book of poems, BOOK OF LONGING, includes both his prose and drawings. Cohen's songs and poems explore spirituality, sexuality, creativity, and complex interpersonal relationships. His awards are as various as inclusion in the Rock and Roll Hall of Fame and as a Grand Officer in the National

Order of Quebec.

BILLY COLLINS (b.1941) was born in New York City. He has published six books of poetry praised for their accessibility, humor, and wit. He has been A Distinguished Professor of English at Lehman College for over thirty years. His many honors include National Endowment for the Arts and Guggenheim Fellowships, and several awards from the Poetry Foundation. He has served two terms as the Poet Laureate of the United States (2001-2003) and was the Poet Laureate of New York from 2004-2006.

JULIA CONNOR (b.1942) was born in Mineola, New York. She served as the Poet Laureate of Sacramento, California from 2005-2008 and has been an instructor at Naropa University's Jack Kerouac School of Disembodied Poetics in Boulder, Colorado. She has published widely in journals and has won numerous fellowships and awards. She teaches writing workshops and master classes in Sacramento, California.

EMILY DICKINSON (1830-1886) was born in Amherst, Massachusetts. After completing her education, she led a reclusive life with most relationships carried out through correspondence. During her lifetime, she published fewer that a dozen poems, most of which were significantly changed by her publishers. Only after her death was she recognized as a major American poet with a prolific body of work. Her poems focus on themes of nature, death, and mortality .

DENISE DUHAMEL (b.1961), born in Woonsocket, Rhode Island, is the author of numerous books and chapbooks known for their combination of poignancy and wit. She is a winner of a National Endowment for the Arts Fellowship and has been included in several volumes of THE BEST AMERCIAN POETRY. She teaches creative writing and literature at Florida International University.

DON EMBLEN (1918-2009) was born in Los Angeles. A teacher and botanist, he was a lifelong writer who produced magazine pieces, scholarly articles, a children's novel, biographies, college textbooks, and TV scripts. Most prominently, he published ten volumes of poetry, ranging from RESTLESS SOLDIERS (1938) to COCK ROBIN (1994). He served as the Poet Laureate of Sonoma County, California.

JEAN FOLLAIN (1903-1971) was born in Canisy in the province of la Manche. He was an author, poet, corporate lawyer, and judge of the High Court. In 1939 he received the Mallarmé Prize and in 1941, the Prix Blumenthal for poets who refused to collaborate with the Vichy government. In 1970, he received the Grand Prize of Poetry from L'Academie Francaise.

CB FOLLETT (b.1936) was born in New York City. She has published four books of poetry, the most recent of which is AND FREDDIE WAS MY DARLING. She was winner of the 2001 National Poetry Book Award from Salmon Run Press and is the publisher/editor of ARCTOS PRESS. From 2001-2008, she published and co-edited RUNES: A Review of Poetry. She lives in Northern California.

REBECCA FOUST (b.1957) was raised in Altonna, Pennsylvania. Her book ALL THAT GORGEOUS, PITILESS, SONG won the Many Mountains Moving Book Award, and two chapbooks, MOM'S CANOE (Texas Review Press, 2009) and DARK CARD (TRP, 2008) won the Robert Phillips Poetry Prize in consecutive years. She lives in Northern California.

VILMA OLSVARY GINZBERG (b.1927) was born in New Jersey. She has published two volumes of poetry, COLORS OF GLASS and MURMURS & OUTCRIES and is co-editor with Doug Stout of the anthology PRESENT AT THE CREATION, a collection on the writing of poetry. As the literary laureate of Healdsburg, California, she created a monthly literary salon that has continued for almost a decade.

DONALD HALL (b.1928), born in New Haven, Connecticut, has published 15 books of poetry, children's books and short stories, and has edited numerous textbooks and anthologies. The recipient of many awards, he was the Poet Laureate of New Hampshire from 1984-1989 and the Poet Laureate of the United States in 2006. He is widely regarded as a plainspoken rural poet in the tradition of Robert Frost. He lives in Danbury, New Hampshire .

JIM HARRISON (b.1937) was born in Grayling, Michigan. His poems about rural America reflect his lifelong connection to the land. He is the author of twenty-three books that include poetry, fiction, non-fiction, and children's literature. He currently lives in a cabin in Michigan, a ranch in New Mexico, and a home in Montana.

JANE HIRSHFIELD (b.1953) was born in New York City. A prize-winning poet, translator, and essayist, she has published six volumes of her own poetry, translations, several anthologies, and a book of essays about poetry. Her poems explore beauty and loss, relatedness and impermanence, and are influenced by her lifelong study of Buddhism. Her many honors include a Poetry Center Award, Guggenheim and Rockefeller Fellowships, and the 70th Academy Fellowship for distinguished poetic achievement by The Academy of American Poets. She lives in Northern California.

SUSAN JACKSON (b.1947), born in Atlanta, Georgia, serves on the Board of Directors of Poets & Writers and the National Arts Club Literary Committee. She lived in France, Belgium, Portugal, and Holland before moving to New Jersey where she currently lives. A widely published poet, she is the author of THROUGH A GATE OF TREES.

WILLIAM KEENER (b.1952) was born in San Francisco. His first co-authored poetry collection, THREE CROWS YELLING (with Bill Noble and Michael Day), won the 2000 Pudding House Prize. His solo chapbook, GOLD LEAF ON GRANITE, won the Anabiosis Press Contest and was published in 2009. An environmental lawyer, much of his work focuses on nature and environmental issues. He lives in Northern California.

JANE KENYON (1947-1995), born in Ann Arbor, Michigan, received her B.A. and M.A. from the University of Michigan, and then moved to Eagle Pond Farm in New Hampshire with her husband, Donald Hall. During her lifetime, she published four books of poetry. At the time of her death in 1995, she was the Poet Laureate of New Hampshire. Books of her poetry, essays, and translations have been published and read widely since her death.

LYNNE KNIGHT (b.1943) was born in Philadelphia and grew up in New York State. Her first collection of poetry DISSOLV-ING BORDERS won a Quarterly Review of Literature Prize. SNOW EFFECTS, a cycle of poems on Impressionist writers, appeared from Small Poetry Press as part of its Select Poetry Se-ries. Her second full-length collection, THE BOOK OF COM-MON BETRAYALS, won the Dorothy Brunsman Award in 2002. She lives in Berkeley, California and teaches writing part-time at two community colleges.

TED KOOSER (b.1939), born in Ames, Iowa, spent most of his working years as an executive in the insurance industry. He has published ten books of poetry and has been awarded some of the most coveted honors in the poetry world. In addition to two Na-tional Endowment of the Arts Fellowships, a Pushcart Prize, and the Stanley Kunitz Prize, he won the Pulitzer Prize in 2004 for DELIGHT & SHADOWS. He has served two terms as the Poet Laureate of the United States. His work has been praised for its clarity and accessibility.

MARILYN KRYSL (b.1942) was raised in Kansas. She has pub-lished four books of short stories and seven books of poetry, known for their blend of humor, political commitment, and lyri-cism. She was the director of the Creative Writing Program at the University of Colorado and has volunteered in many parts of the world including with Mother Teresa's Sisters of Charity in Cal-cutta.

STANLEY KUNITZ (1905-2006), born in Worcester, Massachu-setts, wrote poems until his death at age 100. During his long ca-reer, he received honors including the Pulitzer and Bollingen Prizes, a National Medal of the Arts from President Clinton, and the National Book Award in Poetry. He served as U.S. Poet Lau-reate twice. A mentor to many younger poets, Kunitz taught at Columbia University and was a founder of the Fine Arts Works

Center in Provincetown, Massachusetts and Poets House In New York City.

DORIANNE LAUX (b.1952) was born in Augusta, Maine. After working as a sanatorium cook, a gas station manager, a maid, and a donut holer, she turned seriously to poetry. She is author of FACTS ABOUT THE MOON, WHAT WE CARRY, and AWAKE. She co-authored THE POET'S COMPANION with Kim Addonizio. Among her awards are the Pushcart Prize, Editor's Choice III Award, and a National Endowment for the Arts Fellowship. She lives in Raleigh, North Carolina and teaches at North Carolina State University.

JAY LEEMING (b.1969) was born in Ithaca, New York. His poems have appeared in numerous journals. His first collection of poetry, DYNAMITE ON A CHINA PLATE, was published in 2006. He has been a featured reader at Butler University, the Omega Institute, and the Woodstock Poetry Festival, and recently taught in Devon, England and at the Edinburgh Center for World Spirituality. He lives and teaches in Ithaca, New York.

MARI L'ESPERANCE (b.1961) was born in Kobe, Japan. Her first book, THE DARKENED TEMPLE, won the 2008 Prairie Schooner Book Prize. She also has published an award-winning chapbook. Her work explores personal and national loss, drawing on her Japanese and American roots. She has taught at NYU, Merritt College in Oakland, and the San Francisco Arts Institute. She currently lives in Northern California where she works in social services.

DENISE LEVERTOV (1923-1997) was born in Essex, England. At age 12, she sent some of her poetry to T.S. Eliot who responded with a long letter of encouragement. She moved to the United States in 1945. During the sixties and seventies, she was involved in the anti-war movement and wrote about the suffering of war. She published over thirty books of poetry and several books of prose and translations. She taught at Brandeis, MIT, Tufts, and Stanford. Her honors included the Robert Frost Prize, the Lenore Marshall Prize, and the Lannan Award.

NAOMI RUTH LOWINSKY (b.1944) was born in California to Jewish parents who left Europe to escape persecution. A member of the San Francisco Jung Institute, she is both a practicing analyst and a teacher in the training and public programs. She is the author of two books of poetry as well as of a recent book THE SISTER FROM BELOW that explores her relationship with the muse through both prose and poetry. She lives in the San Francisco Bay Area.

GWENDOLYN MacEWEN (1941-1987) was a Canadian novelist and poet who wrote 26 books. Born in Toronto, Ontario, she left school at 18 to pursue her writing career. She won the Governor General's Award in 1969 for THE SHADOW MAKER, and won a second Governor General's Award for AFTERWORLDS. She served as writer in residence at both the University of Ontario and the University of Toronto. Her visionary and witty work often engaged themes of magic and mythology.

ANTONIO MACHADO (1875-1939), one of Spain's most beloved poets, was born in Seville. A member of the "Generation of '98," his work evolved from an earlier ornate style to a later simplicity. In the years preceding the Spanish Civil War, he wrote of the Spanish countryside and its people, and of the political turmoil tearing his country apart. During his life, he worked as an actor, a translator, a playwright, and a university professor.

WESLEY McNAIR (b.1941) was born in New Hampshire. Sometimes called a poet of place, he has explored the life of New England with humor and telling detail. He has written or edited 18 books, and has been the recipient of fellowships from the Rockefeller, Fulbright, and Guggenheim Foundations. He has appeared in two editions of THE PUSHCRT PRIZE ANNUAL and two editions of BEST AMERICAN POETRY. He is Professor Emeritus and Writer In Residence at the University of Maine in Farmington. He lives in Mercer, Maine.

LISEL MUELLER (b.1924), born in Hamburg, Germany, moved to the United States at age 15. Her many awards include a National Book Award (1981) for THE NEED TO HOLD, the Pulitzer Prize (1997) for ALIVE TOGETHER: NEW & SE-

LECTED POEMS, and a 2002 Ruth Lily Prize. She has taught at the University of Chicago, Goddard College, and Elmhurst College.

KIRSTEN JONES NEFF (b.1966) was born in Palo Alt, California, She blogs online at *Englishcafe.com* and *IndianValleyOrganicFarm.Blogspot.com*. Her chapbook WHEN THE HOUSE IS QUIET won the 2009 Starting Gate Prize from Finishing Line Press and will be published in Spring 2010. She is a founder of Poetry Farm, a monthly reading series in Novato, California.

PABLO NERUDA (1904-1973) was born in Parral, Chile. His unusually prolific life included a career as an internationally recognized poet, a diplomat and a senator representing the Chilean Communist Party. Neruda's extensive poetry includes lush love poems, historical epics of South America, political tracts, and poetry about the land and people of Chile. He was awarded the Nobel Prize in Literature in 1971.

NAOMI SHIHAB NYE (b.1952) was born to a Palestinian father and an American mother. She is the author of numerous books of poetry and has been a Lanaan Fellow, a Guggenheim Fellow, and a Wittner Brenner Fellow. She has traveled three times to the Middle East and Asia for the United States Information Agency to promote peace through the arts. She lives in San Antonio, Texas and is Poetry Editor for THE TEXAS OBSERVER.

LINDA PASTAN (b.1932), born in the Bronx, has written 12 books of poetry and a number of essays. Her many awards include a Pushcart Prize, an Alice Fay di Castagonia Prize (Poetry Society of America) and the 2003 Ruth Lily Poetry Prize. She is known for short poems about family life, aging, death, and the fragility of life. She lives in Potomoc, Maryland.

KATHA POLLITT (b.1949) was born in New York City. A feminist essayist, critic, and poet., she is best known for her column "Subject To Debate" in THE NATION. Her writing explores contemporary feminism, abortion, human rights, the politics of poverty, and U.S. foreign relations. An accomplished poet, she won a National Book Critic's Circle Award in 1983 for ANT-ARCTIC TRAVELLER.

JUDITH PORDON (b. 1954) was born in Atlanta, Georgia. She is the author of two books of poetry and the editor of an online literary poetry anthology CASA POEMA, visited by millions of people each year. In her own work, she explores multicultural and social issues as well as personal relationships. She divides her time between San Diego and Mexico.

CONNIE POST (b.1961) was born in Novato, California. A widely published poet and author of several chapbooks, she was the first Poet Laureate of Livermore, California (2005-2009). During her tenure, she created two popular reading series and wrote a chapbook, IN A CITY OF WORDS, chronicling events in Livermore. She currently hosts another popular Northern California reading series.

MIKLÓS RADNÓTI (1909-1944), born in Budapest, was a poet and translator who wrote notable romantic poetry as well as poems revealing his strong Hungarian identity. Toward the end of his life, he was expelled from Hungarian society for being a Jew. Force--marched to Central Hungary, his life ended in a mass grave. When his body was recovered, his last poems were found on him. These lyrical, poignant poems represent some of the only surviving work composed during the Holocaust.

KATHRYN RIDALL (b.1948) was born in Pittsburgh, Pennsylvania. She came to poetry late in life after a long career as a psychotherapist and university instructor. Published widely, she is the author of the chapbook, THE WAY OF STONES, and editor of WHEN THE MUSE CALLS: POEMS FOR THE CREATIVE LIFE. She lives in the San Francisco Bay Area.

RAINER MARIA RILKE (1875-1926) was born in Prague in the Austro-Hungarian Empire. During his lifetime he lived in Germany, France. Italy, and Switzerland and made spiritually significant journeys to Russia. Known as one of the greatest nineteenth century German language poets, he was particularly interested in the reciprocal relationship between God and the ordinary world. His prose works. LETTERS TO A YOUNG POET and THE NOTEBOOKS OF MALTE LAURIDS BRIGGE, are widely read today.

RUMI (1207-1273), born in Afghanistan, migrated with his family to Konya, Turkey during his youth. Until age 37, Rumi was a brilliant scholar and popular teacher in the dervish learning community of Konya. In 1244, he met Shams of Tabriz, a wandering dervish, who became his beloved teacher and companion. After Sham's disappearance, Rumi's grief and passion produced the ecstatic poetry that is so popular today.

PRIMUS ST. JOHN (b.1939) was born in New York City. He has worked as laborer, gambler, and civil servant. For over thirty years, he has taught at Portland State University. The author of several books of poetry and two anthologies, he has won the Western States Book Award and the Hazel Hall Award for Poetry. Through the National Endowment for the Arts, he helped to create the Poetry in the Schools Program. He lives in Portland, Oregon.

PRATHO SERENO (b.1947) was born in Rochester, New York. She is the author/illustrator of the poetry collection, CAUSING A STIR: THE SECRET LIVES AND LOVES OF KITCHEN UTENSILS, winner of a 2008 Bronze IPPY. Her other publications include CALL FROM PARIS (Word Works Washington Prize for Poetry), and a book of essays, EVERYDAY MIRACLES. She lives in Northern California where she is a Poet in the Schools.

THOMAS R. SMITH (b.1948) is a writer and teacher living in western Wisconsin. His most recent books include WAKING BEFORE DAWN (2007) and KINNICKINNIC (2008). His work has been featured in Garrison Keillor's "The Writer's Almanac" radio program and in U.S. Poet Laureate Ted Kooser's syndicated column, "American Life in Poetry.' He teaches poetry at the Loft Literary Center in Minneapolis.

GARY SNYDER (b.1930), born in San Francisco, is known for his early association with the Beat poets and for his commitment to Buddhism and environmental activism. He has published eighteen books that have been translated into twenty languages. TURTLE ISLAND won the 1976 Pulitzer Prize for poetry. His other awards include The John Hay Award for Nature Writing and the Bollingen Prize. He was elected a Chancellor of the Academy of American Poets in 2003 and teaches English at the University of California, Davis.

WILLIAM STAFFORD (1914-1993) was born in Hutchinson, Kansas. His experience as a conscientious objector during WWII is explored in both his poetry and memoirs. Stafford published his first major book of poetry at 48 and went on to publish 36 books of poetry and prose. He taught at Lewis and Clark College in Portland from 1948-1980. The winner of various awards including the National Book Award and a Western State Achievement Award, he was a Consultant in Poetry to the Library of Congress in 1970.

MARK STRAND (b.1934) was born on Prince Edward Island, Canada. The author of numerous books of poetry, prose, and translation, he is known for his surreal imagery and themes of absence and negation. His many prizes included Fullbright and MacArthur Fellowships, the Bollingen Prize, the Wallace Steven Award, and the Pulitzer Prize in 1999. He served as the Poet Laureate of the United States and has taught at Johns Hopkins, the University of Chicago, and Columbia.

JOSEPH STROUD (b.1943), born in Glendale, California, has written five books of poetry and received a Pushcart Prize and a Witter Bynner Fellowship in Poetry. His poems reveal an intimate relationship with nature and with the Chinese poets Li Po, Tu Fu, and Ho Shan. He divides his time between Santa Cruz, California and a cabin in the Sierra Nevada.

ANNA SWIR, born Anna Swirszczynska, (1909-1984) was raised in Warsaw, Poland. She was a member of the Polish Resistance during the Nazi Occupation in WWII and worked as a nurse during the Warsaw Uprising. She published nine volumes of poetry which explore motherhood, the female body, sensuality, and her experiences during WWII.

WISLAWA SZYMBORSKA (b.1923) was born in Kornik, Poland. A poet, essayist, and translator, she was awarded the Nobel Prize in Literature in 1996. Filled with irony and wit, her poems often grapple with ethical issues. Her poetry has been set to music by Zbigniew Preisner and she is widely read and loved in her native Poland. Among her many awards are the City of Cracow Prize for Literature, the Goethe Prize, and the Polish PEN Club Prize.

JAMES TATE (b.1943) was born in Kansas City, Missouri. His first collection of poems , written while still a student at the University of Iowa Writer's Workshop, strongly influenced his generation of poets. Since then he has published both many books of poetry and various works of prose. His honors include a National Institute of Art and Letters Award for Poetry, Guggenheim Foundation and the National Endowment for the Arts Fellowships, and the Pulitzer Prize. He teaches at the University of Massachusetts in Amherst and is a Chancellor of the Academy of American Poets.

SARA TOLCHIN, pen name Sara Berkeley, (b.1967) grew up in Dublin, Ireland. She has published four collections of poetry, PENN, HOME-MOVIE NIGHT, FACTS AND WATER, and STRAWBERRY THIEF. She has also published a novel SHADOWING HANNAH and a collection of short stories, THE SWIMMER IN THE DEEP BLUE DREAM. She lives with her family in Northern California.

DAVID WHYTE (b.1955) grew up in Yorkshire, England. Trained in Marine Zoology, he worked as a naturalist in the Galapagos. He has written several volumes of poetry that reflect his lifelong connection to nature as well as three books exploring the meaning of work and work-life balance. When not leading workshops in the field of organizational development, he lives in the Pacific Northwest.

JAMES WRIGHT (1927-1980) was born in Martin's Ferry, Ohio. Always lyrical, his poetry shifted from early iambic verse to later free form verse. The subject matter of his poetry showed similar range— from dark personal despair to a luminous appreciation of the world. Wright won the Pulitzer Prize in 1972 for his COLLECTED POEMS. He taught at Hunter College in New York until his death in 1980.

PERMISSIONS

134